Books in a Box:
Lutie Stearns
and the
Traveling Libraries
of Wisconsin

Books in a Box:
Lutie Stearns
and the
Traveling Libraries
of Wisconsin

Stuart Stotts

BIG VALLEY PRESS

For information address: Big Valley Press,
S2104 Big Valley Road, LaFarge, WI. 54639
www.bigvalleypress.com

Publisher Cataloging-in-Publication Data
Stotts, Stuart 1957-
Books in a Box:
Lutie Stearns and the traveling libraries
of Wisconsin/Stuart Stotts
p. cm.
Includes bibliographical references

Summary: From 1895 to 1914, Lutie Stearns established
hundreds of traveling libraries throughout Wisconsin.

ISBN 0976537206
1.Stearns, Lutie, 1866-1943—Biography—Juvenile Literature.
2.Librarians—Biography—Juvenile Literature.
3.Traveling libraries—Wisconsin— History. —Juvenile Literature. I.Title.
Z720.S78 S76   2005
027.4/775—dc22   2005920900

Big Valley Press
First Edition

Printed on Acid Free Paper
Printed in Canada

Cover photos: Wisconsin Historical Society, #29370, 29372, 29377
and Dunn County Historical Society

There is not such a cradle of democracy upon the earth as the Free Public Library, this republic of letters, where neither rank, office, nor wealth receives the slightest consideration.
Andrew Carnegie

Dedicated to librarians everywhere

ACKNOWLEDGEMENTS

I want to thank many people for their help. My first readers graciously offered their time, their suggestions, and their enthusiasm: Carolyn Benson, the Carter family, Kate Edwards, Bobbie Malone, Elizabeth Matson, Maia (Linkcat) McNamara, Linda Mundt, Anna Osborn, Gayle Pachucki, David Rhodes, Mary Taylor, Barbara Tilsen, and my daughters, Cerisa and Calli Obern. Megan Schliesman, Larry Nix, and Michele Besant read the manuscript and generously shared their expertise about libraries and books. I owe special thanks to Christine Pawley for her research and passion for Lutie and libraries. I relied on the wonderful resources, archives, and assistance of the Wisconsin State Historical Society, the Children's Cooperative Book Center, the School of Library and Information Sciences at the University of Wisconsin-Madison, the Wisconsin Reference and Loan Library, the Dunn County Historical Society, and the Madison Public Library. Thanks to Karen Faster for copyediting and Nancy Zucker for book design. And to all the folks at Big Valley Press, you're the best!

Special thanks to many friends for general life support, especially Barbara Chusid, Richard Ely (friend and editor), Charlie Knower, Becky Loy, Bruce Miller, Tom Pease, Marjorie M. Garita Sánchez, Kate Stafford, and everyone in Tongue 'n' Groove. Deep gratitude to my family, Sara, Cerisa, and Calli Obern, as well as my parents and my sisters, for their love and encouragement.

Keep reading!

Stuart Stotts
Madison, Wisconsin
March, 2005

Two girls enjoy the books of a traveling library in 1897.

TABLE OF CONTENTS

Traveling libraries were often tucked in next to brooms, lanterns, or whatever else was for sale in general stores and post offices, like this one in Downsville.

AUTHOR'S NOTE

I first heard about Lutie Stearns from a librarian named Karen Guth, when I was performing in Crandon, Wisconsin. After the concert, she showed me an old wooden traveling library box on display, and she mentioned Lutie. On my drive home, my curiosity grew, as I kept thinking about the story. Over the next few months I researched Lutie's life, and she became a hero to me, for her passion, her persistence, and her courage. Plus, she loved books.

This is a fictionalized biography. I worked from all the facts I could gather, but then I imagined scenes, events, and conversations that would help to make her story come alive. Some material comes directly from her letters and reports, as well as from articles about her in magazines. Any material that is quoted directly is in *italicized* type. I've documented the sources I used in the Bibliography.

There aren't easy answers to questions about how to write a life story. Is it okay to imagine scenes and conversations, or should you just stick with exactly what the documents tell you directly? How do you give the truest picture of a person's life? My answers at this time are here in this book. Still, I wonder. Lutie Stearns was a woman with strong opinions. What would she think?

Lutie Stearns in 1897.

The Gospel of Books

utie Stearns closed her eyes for a moment and then looked out at the people crowded into the small village hall. It was a raw winter night in Wisconsin, and the year was 1901. She saw lumberjacks, farmers, housewives, and children, all waiting patiently. Their clothes were dirty and torn. The ripe smell that comes from people who haven't bathed in weeks hung in the air. Lutie knew that some of her audience had traveled miles through snow-covered forests and on frozen roads to hear what she had to say, and she did not want to disappoint them. She straightened her long brown dress, smiled, and spoke.

"L-l-l-l-ladies and g-g-g-entlemen. Thank you for c-c-coming t-t-tonight to hear about b-b-b-b-ooks."

Lutie took a deep breath and ran her hand over her short, tightly curled hair. She thought, "If I can just get past the beginning, the stutter will probably go away, like it usually does." But she saw the doubt in the eyes of her listeners. She knew that many of them spoke little English, and that her problem was, in a way, the same as theirs: how to be understood.

She began again. "L-l-ladies and gentlemen, n-n-never forget this. Books change lives." She held up a copy of *Uncle Tom's Cabin*. "This book changed history. Books have changed my life, over and over again. And b-b-b-books can change your lives, as well."

She saw a spark of interest in the eyes of an older farmer on her left. In the back, where the wind rattled the windowpanes, two young women craned their necks forward to hear.

Lutie knew how hard people worked just to survive here in northern Wisconsin. Winter was long, the growing season was short, and the farm fields were littered with stumps from the giant white pines that the loggers had felled and sent down the rivers. For farmers and loggers who scratched out a living by the strength in their arms, the sweat on their foreheads, and the occasional help from their neighbors, there was little time to sit and read. With so much work to be done in this harsh land, reading could seem like the worst of all sins: laziness.

A baby cried, and its mother began to nurse it. The crowd was quiet, ready to hear more.

"Books helped our founding fathers, Washington, Jefferson, Adams, to form the ideas that l-l-l-led to our country becoming a d-d-democracy. Books helped Abraham L-L-Lincoln find strength to lead our country in a war for freedom for all m-m-men. Books have carried the m-message of religion down through the years. Reading opens door after door after door. The stories of King Arthur and Odysseus. Poems by Tennyson and Milton and Emily Dickinson. Books about new ways of farming and building and sewing. Most of all, books can help you make up your own m-m-mind about things. Books will tell you how and why and who, each book like a light shining in your heart."

Lutie paused. The fire in the wood stove created an oasis of heat in the room. Someone coughed in the back, and a loud pop echoed as a log shifted in the stove.

"People need and love books," she continued. "I once met a man who fought in the Civil War, where he lost both his arms. He came to the library every month with a bag around his neck to carry books home, so that his mother could read to him. They were particularly interested in books about the life of President Lincoln.

"And only last week, I had a woman tell me of her own pleasure in reading. She and her husband live on a small farm in Vilas County. These are her very words. 'We read aloud most of the time. When he's busy, I read to him. When I'm busy, he reads to me, and that's how we keep going.' Her story is not unique. I have heard of men almost dying of mental starvation in lumber camps, and books are the cure."

She saw a few people nod their heads in agreement, but a husky man in a thick red coat interrupted, with suspicion in his voice. "Books are expensive. What are you trying to sell us?" People nodded to each other at his question.

Lutie smiled kindly. "You are right. Books are expensive. Books are hard to come by. There are no bookstores here."

She waited a moment and then went on. "And that is exactly what I am here to talk to you about tonight. A library. A traveling library, that will bring books to your town, books that you can borrow for free, with only your promise to read them, to take care of them, and to return them. I work for the Wisconsin Free Library Commission, and it is our mission to provide books for you, if your community will provide a place to keep them. Books of all kinds, that everyone can read."

All eyes were on her now, as people leaned forward to catch her words. She watched their faces come alive with curiosity.

A thickly accented voice interrupted her. "Have you books in German?" asked a middle-aged man in patched overalls.

"We have books in Polish, in German, in Finnish, in Swedish. Not as many as I would like, but some for those of you who read in other languages."

A small blond-haired girl seated in the front row spoke up. "Do you have books for girls, too?"

Lutie smiled down at her. "We do. Books about princesses and kings and horses and magic. We have books with drawings, too. Just right for a young lady your age."

People began to talk to each other. Lutie could distinguish some of their questions through the rising murmur of the crowd. "How do we get one of these libraries?" "What does it cost?" "Where would we keep it?"

"May I have your attention, please!" Lutie's voice was strong now, loud enough to be heard over the conversations in the hall. The audience became quiet again.

"I have already spoken with Mr. Lillequist, the proprietor of the store and post office. He will be glad to lend us some counter space for the library."

Lutie watched as smiles of understanding lit up one face after another; people understood that a library would come to their town.

For the next hour, Lutie spoke about books and traveling libraries. Afterward, she mingled with people over homemade muffins, coffee, and apple cider. Before she left, Lutie promised she would bring a library on her next visit.

Lutie left the hall late that night in a horse-drawn sleigh and headed to a hotel in Crandon, nearly ten miles away. Her driver was a fourteen-year-old boy she'd hired earlier that day. Two of the four seats in the sleigh had been removed, and chests of books bound for other towns were piled in their place. The warmth of her reception, her fur coat, and a thick bearskin blanket helped ward off the chill of the winter wind.

Lutie pulled the blanket tighter around her as the sleigh bounced over bumps in the road. "When shall I be done with this stutter?" she thought. "It always gets in the way. Still, it's not as bad as it used to be when I was young." She looked up at the moon shining through the snow-covered trees. She glowed with satisfaction as she anticipated the joy on the faces of the townspeople when the books finally arrived, but she also thought of all the communities that were still without books, and how she intended to visit every one of them.

Write Right!

utie Eugenia Stearns was born on September 13, 1866, in the town of Stoughton, Massachusetts, the youngest of nine sisters and one brother. Her parents were Isaac Holden and Catharine Stearns. One of her sisters named her, and Lutie never knew why that sister chose such an unusual first name.

Lutie always thought of herself as a plain-looking woman. Later in her life, she reflected on her own appearance. *"The advantage to being homely is that you can only look a little better or a little worse than usual."* Her hair was short and curly, she was of medium height, and she wore long dark dresses like most women of her time. She was physically frail; curvature of the spine and stomach problems, which began in childhood, afflicted her for her whole life. She also suffered from skin cancer. But everyone who knew Lutie described her as a bundle of energy who was always ready to work hard.

Her father had been a doctor in the Civil War. When Lutie was five, her family moved to Wisconsin, where her father worked at the Soldiers' Home in Milwaukee. The grounds of the Home were beautiful. Later in her life, Lutie wrote that she spent time *"rowing and wading in the lakes on the grounds, walking down the long shaded lanes with wild flowers in the spring and the birds in the air."* Lutie attended a one-room schoolhouse in Milwaukee for the first years of her education. This is where the trouble with her stutter began.

Lutie attended a one-room schoolhouse, perhaps like this one. However, in 1897, this school in Weston contained a traveling library.

Lutie reached for her pen and felt the sharp crack of a ruler against her left hand. She dropped the pen and watched it slide slowly across her wooden desk to the floor. Her teacher stood behind her left shoulder, towering over the young girl.

"Right hand, Lutie! How many times have I told you? We write with our right hand. Write, right. I should think that would make it easy for you to remember. Use your right hand."

The year was 1874. Lutie Stearns was eight years old and in third grade. She was left-handed, but in those times, many people thought that left-handedness was a bad habit that must be broken. Lutie's wrist stung from the blow, but she clenched her teeth and looked straight ahead at the blackboard without blinking. Some older students in the back rows snickered.

The floorboards creaked as the teacher walked past. From the bookshelf, she chose a copy of a McGuffey Reader, a common school book of the time. "Children, it's time to read. Let's begin with number 2 on page 47. Perhaps Lutie can at least read correctly. Remember, Lutie, we begin on the left side of the page. That should be easy for you to remember." The teacher pointed as she handed the book to Lutie, who knew perfectly well where to begin.

Ever since her teacher had first insisted that Lutie

not use her left hand for writing, Lutie had begun to stammer and stutter. Worse yet, other students imitated her stutter, spitting and drooling and making contorted faces at her on the playground. They laughed when she tried to answer questions in class. Their insults didn't stop her from reading alone, but she hated when she had to speak in front of the class.

"At one t-t-t-time, h-h-h-owever, H-H-Henry wanted a g-g-g-g-grammar, in order to j-j-j-join a c-c-class in that s-s-study…"

Behind her, someone laughed. Lutie kept on. "… and his m-m-m-mother c-c-c-could n-n-n-not furnish h-h-h-him with the m-m-money to buy it."

The teacher interrupted. "Well, that's enough from you. At this rate, we won't finish the passage until Friday. Franklin, would you continue?"

Lutie handed the book to the curly haired boy next to her, who smiled and sat up straight as he read. "He was very much troubled about it, and went to bed with a heavy heart, thinking what could be done."

Lutie slumped in her seat, her face flushed. She glared at Franklin and thought, "I'm one of the best readers here. And I love books, not like some of these kids." She looked out the window at the sunny early spring day, as Franklin's voice trailed off. She imagined herself walking along the creek near her home, listening to frogs as she picked mint and cattails.

For her next two years in the small country school, Lutie struggled with teachers who insisted that she write with her right hand. Her stutter grew worse. When Lutie was 10, her father became a health officer for the city of Milwaukee, and she attended the 11th Ward School, which, unlike the one-room schoolhouse, had separate classes for each grade. However, in fifth, sixth, and seventh grade, her problems with teachers continued. Lutie was seen as willful and rebellious, and her seventh-grade teacher had even said that she *"couldn't wait to get my clutches on that Lutie Stearns,"* in order to teach her obedience and discipline. Lutie fought a yearlong battle with this teacher, who threatened and ridiculed Lutie for her left-handedness and her stutter. Lutie was often absent, overcome by stress and what she called a *"nervous condition."* Although she loved to learn, school was torture.

Lutie waited for her first day of eighth grade to begin. She sat near the back of the room by an open window. A familiar dread filled her body as she watched her new teacher survey the students.

Lutie's jaw ached, and her stomach churned. Her teacher, Miss Burr, stood in front of the blackboard as she checked the attendance, listed the school rules, and outlined subjects the class would study this year. Although Miss Burr seemed friendly enough, Lutie feared the inevitable moment when she would ask Lutie to speak or read aloud, and her stutter would lead to another year of agony. Lutie didn't have to wait long.

"Now, class, let's see how well you read," said Miss Burr. "We will give Charles Dickens a try this morning." She handed a book to a girl in the front row, who began, "It was the best of times, it was the worst of times..."

Miss Burr walked up and down the rows of wooden desks, asking first one student then another to read parts of the story. Some read easily, while others struggled, pausing and stumbling over unknown words. Lutie lost track of who was reading, as her palms grew damp with sweat, and her stomach tightened.

Finally, Miss Burr stood over Lutie and handed her the book, pointing to a passage. Lutie began. "It was the D-D-D-Dover R-R-R-Road that l-l-l-lay, on a Friday n-n-night late in N-N-November." She looked up at Miss Burr.

"Continue here, please," said Miss Burr, pointing to a different spot. Lutie read, "W-w-w-with d-d-d-drooping heads and t-t-tremulous t-t-tails, they m-m-mashed their way through the thick m-m-m-mud, floundering and st-st-st-stumbling between whiles as if they were f-f-falling to p-p-pieces at the l-l-larger j-j-joints." She stopped and heard laughter all around her.

" I see," said Miss Burr, as she took the book and walked back to the chalkboard. "Well, thank you, Lutie. You certainly are very advanced in your ability to recognize words, and no doubt, also understand their meaning. I wonder if you might be willing to take this note to the office for me. I neglected to send it earlier. Would you be so kind?"

Lutie rose to her feet, trudged to the front and took the note from Miss Burr's hand. As she walked into the hallway, she heard Miss Burr say, "Now, class, you each must..." but Lutie could hear no more as she closed the door behind her.

The following day and all throughout the year, when Lutie read or spoke, every student in the classroom was silent.

After Lutie graduated from the 11th Ward School, she attended Cass Street High School. She walked four miles to and from school every day. Lutie made good friends in the school and became a very good student.

During this time, Lutie's father deserted their family. Later in her life, Lutie wrote about his leaving: *"He went to Michigan where he obtained a* divorce *from my faithful mother, then went back to Massachusetts where he later remarried."*

This could have been a devastating event, but Lutie's mother held the family together. Lutie later remembered, *"during this tragic experience my mother never once referred to my father's totally unexpected departure, nor in all of her later years did she ever make mention of the desertion…she did not let it affect her usual cheeriness and her interest in her family."*

All her life Lutie talked about her admiration for her mother, and it is easy to trace the roots of Lutie's own persistence and cheerfulness back to her mother's influence. After her father left, Lutie assumed more responsibility for supporting the family. Lutie also chose to use her mother's last name instead of her father's.

In 1883, Lutie graduated from Cass Street High School. She enrolled in college to get her teaching certificate. Two years later, Lutie had graduated and was ready for her own classroom.

What, No Books?

understand that we have n-n-no books?"

Lutie Stearns stood in the front of her classroom looking at the 72 fourth-graders who would be her students for the coming year. Eight children sat on chairs in the aisles, because there weren't enough desks. Today was her first day teaching at the 13th Ward School in Milwaukee. It was 1886, and Lutie was 20 years old. She had finished college the previous spring, and her pay was $45 per month.

One of the students, a sandy-haired boy in overalls and worn boots, raised his hand. "Well, Miss Stearns, there is a book."

"A book?" she said. "Ah yes, I forgot. I had heard that there m-m-might be one book."

"Yes, miss. We have a primer for the room."

"O-o-one b-b-b-b-ook for all 72 of y-y-you?"

If he took any notice of her stutter, he did not dare

show it. "Well, yes, but we share it as we can, miss."

"Indeed."

The sun beat down through the windows, and the room was heating up. Some of the students shifted uneasily in their seats and looked around the crowded room. Lutie glanced at the doorway and thought, "Heaven forbid there should be a fire. We'd never all get out in time."

Lutie's students came from poor families, most of whom had recently emigrated from Germany. Often German was the only language spoken in their homes. For a moment, Lutie felt overwhelmed. "Without books," she thought, "without enough desks, without knowing much English, it's a wonder these children have learned anything at all. Still, I didn't come here to waste their time, or mine. If they need books, then I will figure out how to get them."

Later that month, Lutie sent home notices to parents that she would give stereopticon lectures, which were like slide shows, on Germany. Parents, children, aunts, uncles, and neighbors crowded into the school gymnasium in the evenings to see projected pictures of their native country. She charged a small admission for each show. No one seemed to mind when Lutie stuttered during the talks. Her audience was certainly familiar with what it meant to suffer from language difficulties.

After several lectures, she had collected $75. She immediately ordered magazines she knew her students would like: *St. Nicholas, Wide Awake, Harper's Young People,* and *Youth's Companion.* She made shelves in her room from old soapboxes and filled them with books borrowed from friends. And she went to the library.

Later in her life, Lutie wrote about getting books for her students. *"Every Thursday night after school I would take three boys and six market baskets and travel by horse car to the Public Library, located over Espenhain's Dry Goods Store on the corner of Grand Avenue and Fourth Street. For each child two books were chosen: one of wholesome fiction, the other along lines through which the child might discover his life interest. I pursued this plan for the two years and two months I spent as a teacher."*

Lutie's students had plenty of books now.

Lutie taught for over two years, bringing books to her students every week. These weekly visits to the library caught the attention of the library staff, and in 1888, Lutie was hired by the library. As Lutie remembered, *"I visited the schools, told stories to the children to interest them in books, and invited their teachers to come to the library to select them. As I recall, I worked up a circulation of more than 98,000 volumes in the schools."*

Lutie worked there for nine years, for $60 per month. She lived with her family in Milwaukee. Through these years of teaching and library work, Lutie helped to support her mother and some of her sisters.

In 1891 Lutie joined the newly formed Wisconsin Library Association, which was created to promote the use and growth of libraries in the state. At the time, Wisconsin had only 35 free public libraries, although a few communities had subscription libraries, where people paid to borrow books.

Lutie was also a member of the American Library Association. In 1894, at an ALA conference, Lutie gave a passionate speech to other librarians on the importance of books for children. At the time, many libraries didn't allow children younger than twelve to take out books. Lutie spoke before a large crowd and stuttered on almost every word. By the time she finished, she was nearly in tears with embarrassment, but the audience rose and applauded, for her courage as much as for her message.

Lutie made a new friend, Frank Hutchins, through the Wisconsin Library Association, which he had helped to found. He was a soft-spoken but determined man, with a short beard and intense

WISCONSIN HISTORICAL SOCIETY. #29375

Frank Hutchins
worked with Lutie
for many years to
create traveling
libraries.

eyes. Frank had helped start the Wisconsin State
Forest Department, and originated the idea of
Easter Seals for the Anti-Tuberculosis Association.
Frank was the school library clerk in the
Department of Public Instruction at Madison. He
had helped to support the library in his hometown
of Beaver Dam, where he worked as the newspaper
editor. Like Lutie, he was convinced that books had
the power to change people's lives. For the next 13
years, Frank Hutchins would be Lutie's partner in
promoting libraries.

Throughout most of the 1890s an economic depression gripped the country. Disease, poverty, and dangerous working conditions were widespread. Many schools were neglected and overburdened, and some children worked long hours in hazardous factory jobs. Lutie, Frank, and many others were shocked by the miserable conditions of poor people's lives. They believed that society could be improved if government helped people through programs and education. Today, we call members of this social movement "Progressives."

In 1893, Lutie and Frank attended a library conference in Chicago where a librarian from New York State named Melvil Dewey spoke. Dewey is remembered today as the inventor of the "Dewey Decimal System," which libraries use to catalog books. However, Melvil Dewey also helped to create the first traveling libraries in the country. Lutie and Frank listened as Dewey described the system of traveling libraries in New York State. They smiled at each other. Now they had an idea that could put their beliefs into action. Through traveling libraries they could help spread knowledge and wisdom throughout the state, improving lives one book at a time.

Capitol Ideas

utie, Frank Hutchins, and James Stout, a state senator from Menomonie, sat in the Capitol in Madison, Wisconsin, in 1894. Their voices echoed against the walnut walls and marble floors of the small meeting room.

"I tell you," said Lutie, "we m-m-must p-p-p-push for it n-now. There is no sense in d-d-d-delaying. This bill is incomplete, but it is a start. People n-n-need books, and the L-l-l-l-legislature has a responsibility to all its citizens."

"The price of ignorance is high," Frank said. "Our country and our state can only be great if people are informed enough to make wise decisions about their own lives and about the government itself."

James Stout looked back and forth between Lutie and Frank. He admired their intensity, and he shared their values. Senator Stout had made a fortune in logging in northern Wisconsin before being elected to the state Senate. He was wealthy, but he cared about people who were less fortunate, and, like Lutie and Frank, he believed that education could help cure poverty.

He remembered when they had approached him months earlier with the idea of traveling libraries for Wisconsin. They wanted him to introduce a bill to create and fund the Wisconsin Free Library Commission.

At that initial meeting their idea appealed to him, but he suggested that they proceed slowly and deliberately. "This is a worthy concept," he said, "which may benefit many people. But we must be certain that the bill is well written, and that we have the support of key agencies in the state. It does not pay to build a house without first making a strong foundation."

Lutie and Frank had gone to work. They gathered copies of library legislation from Massachusetts and New Hampshire, and based the Wisconsin bill on the best ideas from both of those states. They talked to other legislators and administrators in state organizations. And now, after months of work, they felt they were ready.

James Stout rubbed his forehead and closed his eyes for a long moment. Then he sat up and spoke forcefully. "I believe that you are both correct. The time is right. We have the support of the State

Senator James Stout helped to pass the legislation to fund traveling libraries, and started his own system in Dunn County.

WISCONSIN HISTORICAL SOCIETY, #29376

Historical Society, the University, and the Department of Public Instruction. By the way, that was very wise of you, Miss Stearns, to gather such a broad range of supporters."

"We m-m-m-must keep this organization as far from p-p-politics as we can, Senator Stout," Lutie said. "By creating a wide constituency, it will be harder to d-d-defeat."

Senator Stout smiled. "Had you been a man, Miss Stearns, you would have made a fine senator. You are a hard person to say 'no' to. I shall introduce the bill as soon as I can speak with a few of my colleagues in the Senate. I know where to begin. And I'm owed a few favors, as well."

"Senator," said Lutie, "the people deserve no less. It is only from educated citizens that true d-d-d-democracy can progress. As Horace Mann said, 'Had I the power I would scatter libraries over the whole l-l-land as a sower sows his wheat.' This is the work we can now begin."

Frank grinned. "As I have said before, because Miss Stearns wants it and believes in it, let us work for a Library Commission."

In 1895, the Legislature and Governor William Upham created the Wisconsin Free Library Commission, to support and expand libraries in Wisconsin. The Legislature also authorized $500 for two years' worth of expenses, such as travel, printing, and postage. Lutie Stearns and Frank Hutchins were appointed to the board of directors. The Milwaukee Public Library gave Lutie some release time to do the secretarial work of the Commission and to travel to communities without libraries. Now the real work of creating traveling libraries could begin.

Dunn County

ames Stout's hometown of Menomonie in Dunn County had a fine public library with many shelves of books, but the 16,000 people who lived in the county borrowed only 3,000 books a year. That wasn't good enough for Senator Stout. People wanted to read, but because of poor dirt roads, distance, and winter weather, they couldn't travel in from the countryside often enough to exchange books regularly. When Lutie and Frank first approached him, he saw that traveling libraries could solve this problem.

After the legislation passed, Frank and Lutie helped Senator Stout to create a system for Dunn County. Stout bought 500 books with his own money. Together they chose the most popular books of the time: classic and contemporary novels, travel books, and biographies. They included children's books, cookbooks, picture books, and books about

TRAVELING LIBRARY BROCHURE 1897

The first traveling libraries are ready to go out to the stations around Dunn County.

history and science. They wanted books that would appeal to *"the busy housewife, the farmer, and mechanic, and the studious men and women."*

The 500 books were divided up into 16 small libraries of about 30 books each. A pamphlet explained how traveling libraries worked. *"Each library was put up in a strong book case which had a shelf, double doors with a lock and key, a record book for loans, printed copies of the few simple rules, borrowers' blanks and so complete a line of equipment that it could be set up anywhere on a table, a box or a counter and managed as an independent library...it was so simple that any intelligent person could operate it after five minutes of explanation."*

James Stout made basic agreements with people in each community that wanted a library. They had to establish a local group to be responsible for the library, and find a volunteer librarian. They had to take good care of the books. People who destroyed or damaged books must be fined. The books had to be available for free, and the library could be exchanged when the community was ready for a new collection. The community had to pay $1 every time they traded the collection, but, in exchange, Stout would cover transportation, book repairs, and other expenses

Libraries were delivered to the first 16 towns in May 1896. Other communities in the county soon wanted libraries as well, so Stout bought ten more, then another nine. People wanted more children's books, so Stout increased the size of the libraries by adding more books for children. In each library box, he included magazines that did not have to be returned.

Many books from that time are still popular today: *Oliver Twist, Black Beauty, Treasure Island, Sherlock Holmes,* Shakespeare's plays, and books by Louisa May Alcott such as *Little Women.* Other books circulated in the libraries are no longer widely read, such as *Helen's Baby, Story of a Bad Boy, Dab Kinzer, Little Smoke,* and *The Electrical Boy,* although in the late 1890s they were among the most requested. There were non-fiction books, such as *The Wisconsin Farm Institute Bulletin* and *Boston Cookbook.* American history books were also in demand. Many of the readers were recent immigrants to the United States, and they wanted to learn the story of their new country.

Lutie and Frank Hutchins visited Dunn County several times to help with the new system and to learn firsthand how it worked. Some of the towns there had reputations for being disorderly and violent. Frank Hutchins wrote about one village he visited in the early stages of the traveling libraries.

"Even rough men acknowledged the value for good literature. At one hamlet where I inquired about a

neighboring four corners, I was told, 'It is useless to go there for it's a regular hell hole.' I visited it, however, and found it included a store, saloon, railway station, blacksmith shop, and a dozen houses. The farmers about were poor and some of them coarse and rough. The storekeeper had received a scant education but he was a prompt reliable businessman and after a time talked quite freely. He said, 'My mother died when I was quite young, my father was a drunkard, and I had a hard time when I was a boy. I had a chance for a few years to get books from a public library, and they furnished me the pleasantest hours I had. I have been pretty rough and our place here is tough. Last Saturday night there was a dance, and the boys filled up with whiskey, and the girls stood around and made fun of them. I believe that if they would read good books, it would put a stop to that kind of thing, and I will take the library and make the boys and girls read the books.' He was as good as his word, and the circulation of his library was double that of the one left in his scoffing neighbor's community."

The library system of Dunn County was a successful beginning for the Wisconsin Free Library Commission. At the same time, smaller experiments were tried in Wisconsin Rapids, Tomahawk, and Chippewa County.

In 1897, the Legislature granted the Commission
$4,000 per year, enough to cover the cost of hiring
employees. Senator James Stout joined the
Commission board. Lutie left her job in Milwaukee,
and she and Frank Hutchins became the paid staff
of the Commission. Lutie's pay that first year was
$100 per month. One of her responsibilities was to
organize new libraries and to oversee the traveling
library department. Frank Hutchins and Lutie
Stearns took the lessons learned in Dunn County
and began to apply them around the state.

A post office, like this one in Colfax, was a
typical spot to place a traveling library.

Company Town

utie rode into the little town of Niagara, in northern Wisconsin, in the front seat of a wagon pulled by four horses. She sat next to the driver, Mr. Sebranek, who was delivering barrels of flour and sugar as well as other goods to the general store. He had been only too happy to accept Lutie as a passenger from the station in Quinnesec, Michigan, which Lutie had reached on the train from Marinette, Wisconsin. As his wagon bounced and jostled over the narrow rugged forest road, he entertained Lutie with stories of the North Woods and its inhabitants. At one point, a fallen tree that blocked the road stopped the wagon, and Lutie waited while Mr. Sebranek sawed the trunk in two and moved it out of their way.

When they finally pulled up in front of the general store, he came around and helped her out of the wagon.

"Miss Stearns," he said, offering her a hand, "welcome to Niagara. The whole town is owned by the Kimberly and Clark Paper Company, as I mentioned to you, and I think you may find lots of folks who wouldn't mind some books to ease their days and nights as well as folks who wouldn't mind helping out. But if I were you, I'd avoid Mr. Olson, the postmaster. He doesn't seem to have a hard-working bone in his body, if you know what I mean, and I can't imagine he'd be interested in anything that means more work."

Lutie handed the driver 25 cents as payment. "Thank you, Mr. Sebranek, for your advice and for the r-r-ride on your wagon. The p-p-post office is often the preferred place for a library, as it is central to every town, but there are always other options."

"Good luck to you, Miss Stearns. I'll be leaving tomorrow afternoon, if you have finished your business and want a ride out."

"We shall see how the work progresses. Good day, Mr. Sebranek."

Lutie picked up her suitcase and walked toward the hotel. She admired the handsome cottages along the street, and the well kept stores. She also noticed that there were several empty storefronts, any one of which might be perfect for a library.

Lutie found a room at the hotel and left her bag-

WISCONSIN HISTORICAL SOCIETY, #29377

Lutie rode into hundreds of small towns looking to place a library. Here in Boyceville the library was located in the second building on the left.

gage. She went to the paper company office, and after a bit of explaining, found herself face to face with the manager, Mr. Ryan. He wore a red sweater and had short blond hair and a thick beard. He looked Lutie up and down, appraising her and her mission with a cool eye.

"Our offer is simply this, sir," said Lutie. "With a p-p-payment of $50, the Free Library Commission will provide two libraries every year, each with 100 books, for a period of five years. We put in the b-b-b-best editions available, and the $50 secures the use of $1000 worth of books."

Mr. Ryan ignored her stutter. "$50 is a lot of money, Miss Stearns," he replied. "We run a tight operation here, without much to spare."

"The m-m-m-money can come from village taxes, from fund-raising events, or from individuals who want to contribute, as well as from your company. In fact, we ask that each community form a library board made up of 10 individuals who will oversee the books. These people will often contribute. For you, it seems a small price to pay to help the w-w-workers you depend on. And I think you can see how reading provides wholesome entertainment, an alternative to the d-d-drinking and fighting that can become such a problem in these isolated towns."

"I have heard of these libraries, I guess. Perhaps the cost could be covered by charging a small rental fee for each book?"

"You are thinking of subscription libraries, where people pay to b-b-borrow books. Such libraries do not fit with our mission. There must be n-n-no charge for borrowing. We receive occasional inquiries as to whether we will permit a charge of 5 cents to be made for each reader's card. This cannot be done because it might keep some child from receiving books. Five cents seems like a small amount, but children do not come by it easily. Nor do some adults, for that matter."

Mr. Ryan looked down at his desk for a moment. Then he turned again toward Lutie. "Miss Stearns, I can see the value in providing books for our town. If you can find 10 citizens to be on your library board, our company will pay $25. You must find others to pay the rest."

Lutie nodded. "It is also helpful to have a central place where the books can be available."

Mr. Ryan's eyes narrowed, and he cocked his head. Suddenly he grinned.

"You know what you want, and you don't quit until you have it, do you, Miss Stearns? Well, we do have a small building that was a doctor's office. It is empty now, and we could let you use it to house the collection."

"Sir, your offer is fair and generous. I will find the rest of the money and the people to form the library board. Perhaps you would like to be the chairman, Mr. Ryan?"

"Miss Stearns, I think that my assistant, Mr. Kloiber, would be glad to fill that role. You may tell him so on your way out."

"Thank you, sir, for your time. I shall return when I have found the m-m-members and the money."

Lutie spent the rest of the day talking with people in Niagara. The schoolteacher said she would be glad to watch over the books, and two men from the stable agreed to be part of the library board. Each contributed a dollar. The owner of the general store joined and contributed, and four women, mothers with children, also agreed to join the board. By the following morning, Lutie had recruited 10 board members and collected the remaining $25.

As Mr. Sebranek had predicted, the postmaster had no interest in the project. Perhaps more surprising, the local minister objected to the library books, as he was opposed to the reading of novels and other "light literature." He felt that the Bible and related spiritual books were all that any person needed to read. He and Lutie exchanged honest but civil views on the subject.

Lutie left his church undeterred. She returned to Mr. Ryan's office in the afternoon with news of her success, and with an agreement that she would bring the books the following month, at which time she would meet with the library board to discuss the operation of the traveling library. She also planned to give an evening talk then to area residents, to promote the library and to explain how to use it.

Lutie rode back to Quinnesec with Mr. Sebranek. The road was muddy from a morning downpour, and more than once he had to push the wagon out of ruts while Lutie held the horses' reins. Lutie listened politely to his stories, but she was already thinking of the next town she planned to visit.

During her nearly 20 years with the Wisconsin Free Library Commission, Lutie spent a good part of her time organizing towns and villages to host libraries. She was often discouraged. Local politics could be unpredictable and were frequently driven by personal grudges and pettiness. People were often unreliable and wouldn't do what they had promised. Some thought that libraries weren't worth the cost. Others had little regard for reading and learning; they believed that life was about working hard, and books were a waste of time.

But Lutie never gave up. Even when she met with failure, she would return and try again. In one of her reports, she wrote, *"The desire to have a good influence and a decent place to go, instead of the many saloons and dance halls, led me to visit one community no less than 12 times before I could get the town president, also owner of a dance hall, to appoint a library board."*

Lutie spread libraries like Johnny Appleseed spread apple trees. From the manufacturing centers of Kenosha and Racine to the lumber camps of the North Woods, Lutie started traveling libraries in every community that would accept one. She looked at maps and talked with people in every area she visited to determine where libraries might be needed. No community was too small for her to visit.

Over the years, Lutie recruited hundreds of volunteers to take responsibility for traveling libraries. However, her ultimate goal was to help communities create and sustain permanent library buildings. When a town was large enough and had shown enough interest, she would often help its citizens to apply for funds from Andrew Carnegie to construct a library. Andrew Carnegie was a wealthy industrialist who, later in his life, began funding libraries around the United States. Between 1901 and 1915, more than 60 Wisconsin municipalities received Carnegie grants to build libraries. (Many of these Carnegie library buildings are still in use today.) Lutie helped with many towns' applications, and she always did her best to attend the cornerstone dedication ceremony of every library, where she could celebrate the beautiful new community institution that had grown from a simple collection of books in a box.

Bearskin Blanket

utie sat writing in the downstairs lobby of a small hotel, a woodstove warming her feet. A fly buzzed slowly overhead. She formed her words deliberately and neatly as she detailed the events of the last few days in a report. She put down her pen and paused to read what she had written so far.

"We left the boxes at the schoolhouse and arranged for a meeting of parents and children in the afternoon two days later. The curiosity of the children was greatly excited by the teacher's acceptance of the suggestion not to reveal the nature of the contents of the boxes.

When we returned for the meeting, we found the schoolhouse crowded with men, women, and children, five of the latter being babes brought by their mothers. There were, however, more men than women in the audience. Every pupil was present for the first time since the opening day. A number of women walked miles to the meeting, the farm horses being away at logging camps.

The boxes were opened when all were assembled. Nearly all of the books were new, and looked fresh and inviting. I gave a brief talk about the books, explaining from when they came, how they themselves were paying for them through the county taxes, and the method by which the books could be drawn and exchanged."

Lutie had seen this situation played out many times, and she was always delighted to be part of it. Excitement filled the room, especially when the children were bursting with the anticipation of a surprise.

Last month, in Beecher Lake, she had arranged a meeting attended by six of the 12 families who lived scattered throughout the surrounding woods. Lutie didn't mind the small numbers of people who had come. What mattered was that people could get books.

A father there had picked up an American history book. He thumbed through the pages carefully, and then gently laid it back down in the chest.

"Miss Stearns," he said. "How much would such a book cost?"

"I believe that this particular book was 82 cents," Lutie replied.

Even a very small post office, like this one in
Louisville, could house a traveling library.

"I would love to have such a thing," he said. "But it will probably be a few years to save that much."

Lutie's heart went out to the man, and if she could have, she would have simply given him the book, as a reward for loving it so much. Instead she said, "Sir, this is the beauty of a library. You can bring this and many other wonderful books into your home, and it will cost you nothing. All you must do is return them when you have finished."

The man smiled, and took the book after filling out a borrower's form.

Lutie looked at the two chests of books by the doorway, brought inside to get out of the snow. She had noticed that several of the books needed repair. Some pages were ripped, and two covers hung by threads. The Library Commission lent the books, but also repaired damaged ones. That took money, of course. Lutie remembered that she needed to write yet another letter to the Legislature, pleading for more funds so that the Commission could hire another person to help with the traveling libraries. How could they expect one woman to cover the whole state, especially when the need was so great?

But in the meantime, the books must be repaired and transported, again and again. To remind people to take good care of the books, Lutie passed out bookmarks with this message.

Stout
Free Traveling Library
BOOK MARK

"Once on a time," a Library Book was overheard talking to a little boy who had just borrowed it. The words seemed worth recording and here they are:

"Please don't handle me with dirty hands. I should feel ashamed to be seen when the next little boy borrowed me.

Or leave me out in the rain. Books can catch cold as well as children.

Or make marks on me with your pen or pencil. It would spoil my looks.

Or lean on me with your elbows when you are reading me. It hurts.

Or open me and lay me face down on the table. You wouldn't like to be treated so.

Or put in between my leaves a pencil or anything thicker than a single sheet of thin paper. It would strain my back.

Whenever you are through reading me, if you are afraid of losing your place, don't turn down the corner of one of my leaves, but have a neat little Book Mark to put in where you stopped, and then close me and lay me down on my side so that I can have a good comfortable rest.

Remember that I want to visit a great many other little boys after you are through with me. Besides, I may meet you again some day, and you would be sorry to see me looking old and torn and soiled. Help me to keep fresh and clean, and I will help you to be happy."

Still musing, Lutie gazed at the doorway, where her fur-lined muskrat coat hung. "My faithful companion," she thought. "How else could I survive these winters?" Lutie had worn out three similar coats in the course of her travels.

She shivered and moved closer to the stove. A thick, furry, black bearskin lay folded next to the chests of books. She liked to throw it over herself as she rode in a sleigh or a buggy, especially when the temperature was below zero.

With a smile, Lutie reached into her bag and pulled out a folded piece of paper. A librarian friend of Lutie's, Mrs. Anna W. Evans, had written a poem about Lutie's winter dressing habits. Lutie read it to herself and laughed quietly.

"There is a woman named Stearns;
Her living she easily earns,
By driving around
When the snow's on the ground,
Though the danger she never discerns.

She dons a coat of black hair;
A cap is next put on with care;
She looks like a man
But to tell you ne'er can
If the product be woman, or bear.

Now if in her drives through the brush
A bruin should come out with a rush,
Would the woman hug the bear
Or the bear hug the air
Or which would be lost in the crush?

Would the bear barely hug the bold jade?
Or the bearskin propelled by the maid
Hug the bear? Or the hair
Of the bear would she tear
Or her own, as the price to be paid?"

"I've seen my share of bears," she thought, "though none has ever attacked me." Lutie refolded the paper and put it away. "Bears, elk, deer, the occasional badger. Every kind of wild creature. And plenty of wild men and women in those isolated towns. Drinking, brawling, fighting. In the end, I think it is the book that will civilize wilderness, not the plow or the axe or the gun."

The innkeeper came in and added a log to the stove. Outside, the wind howled. Lutie threw a shawl over her shoulders, took the pen in her left hand, and returned to writing her report.

A traveling library was made to be self-contained, with shelves, books, borrowers cards, and the rules printed on the door. This library was located in the Daudig family's home.

Checking In,
Checking Out

utie was tired, and the bouncing of the stagecoach only drove the fatigue deeper into her bones. She stared out the window through the early spring sunshine at a hillside littered with treetops and huge stumps, clear-cut by lumberjacks the previous winter. Sprouts of green poked up through the downed tops and branches. "Will there be any big trees left when the loggers have finished?" she wondered to herself.

In her travels through northern Wisconsin, Lutie had seen a thousand similar hillsides. She had brought books to many lumber camps and was familiar with the difficulties and dangers that lumberjacks faced. They worked hard, and the threat of death was never far away.

"I feel as tired as a lumberjack myself," thought

Lutie. Nearing the end of a two-week trip, she had visited 15 communities. The trip had been like the hilly, up-and-down terrain she traveled, with successes and failures, often in the course of the same day.

Lutie had worked for the Commission for more than 10 years, and her job title was now "Organizer of Traveling Libraries." Frank Hutchins had retired in 1904, and a year later Senator Stout left his position on the Library Commission board. Lutie carried on the work herself, without the help of her early associates.

With the growth of so many libraries around Wisconsin, her job had changed. She started fewer traveling libraries, and spent more time overseeing the ones already established. Although Lutie did much of her work from her office in Madison, she still traveled a great deal.

Just yesterday she had visited a library in Cumberland, a new brick building Andrew Carnegie funded. When Lutie walked in, she was dismayed to discover that no one had paid any attention to decorating the interior. One little cactus plant stood by the desk. There were no paintings, no pictures, and no sign of color beyond the shelves, the books, and the bare white walls. When Lutie suggested that some decoration might improve the atmosphere, the librarian replied, "We have books, miss. What

This traveling library provided a comfortable spot to read at the back of a store in Browning.

else is a library for?" Lutie had gone straight to a leader of the local woman's club to ask that their members do something to alter the situation. Lutie planned to return in a few months, to see if any changes had been made.

The stagecoach slowed. The driver called to Lutie, who was his only passenger. "We'll stop for an hour or so, Miss Stearns. I believe you have some business here, and the horses can use a rest. I can help you with your box when you need."

Lutie walked down the short main street toward the store where she had left a library six months ago. The door clattered as she entered the dim store. The proprietor looked up from behind the counter.

"Mr. Mullinghurst, my name is Lutie Stearns. It is a pleasure to see you again. I left a traveling library with you on my last trip through, and I've brought a new one to exchange, if you like."

"Miss Stearns. Ah, yes, the library."

"Have the books been well used?"

"Well, I couldn't say. They're in the back of the store. My children have been in charge of them, as I've been very busy lately. I do see folks walking in and out with books sometimes."

Lutie walked to the rear of the store, where her fears were confirmed. The traveling library chest lay open, with books piled inside like apples in a crate. There were no shelves, and the borrower cards were scattered on the floor.

Lutie marched up to the front of the store. "Sir, how old are your children?"

He looked down at the floor. "Eva is 6 and Stephen is 8. But they do love books."

"Sir, I am afraid that this is unacceptable. Our books must be well taken care of."

"As I said, miss, I'm very busy, and I'm not much of a reader myself…"

"I think it best if I find another place for the library. Thank you."

Lutie could barely contain her anger as she walked out of the store and across the street to the stable. She remembered that Mr. Jorgenson was the owner of the stable, as well as the president of the library board. But when Lutie attempted to speak with him about the condition and placement of the books, he replied, "I'm not sure this town is ready for a library, Miss Stearns. And Mr. Mullinghurst does the best he can. You should be grateful to have a place at all."

Lutie left the stable and looked up and down the street. On one side, she saw a wood shop, a butcher shop, a funeral parlor, and a dress shop. She began to walk slowly.

"This might be worth a try," thought Lutie, as she approached the dress shop. She noticed the clean glass and the neat arrangement of colorful fabrics in the window.

Lutie opened the door and two cheerful young women who sat sewing and cutting at a table greeted her.

"Hello, may we help you?" said one of the women as she rose from her seat.

"Good day. You have a lovely shop here." Lutie paused. "My name is Lutie Stearns, and I work for the Wisconsin Free Library Commission."

"A pleasure to meet you. My name is Ruth Swenson, and this is Ingeburg Larson. Are you the woman who brought the free books to the store?"

"Yes, I am. Do you like the books?"

"Yes, I do. We both do. But I think we have read them all. Have you brought more?"

"I have. But I am afraid that I am looking for a new home for the traveling library. Mr. Mullinghurst and his young children do not seem up to the task of caring for the collection." Lutie looked around at the store and saw the tidy shelves filled with cloth and the carefully organized rows of thread and buttons. "I was wondering if you might be interested in housing the books?"

"Do you mean, have the books here?" Ingeburg asked.

"Precisely. I do not think Mr. Mullinghurst will miss them. And I can see that you both take pride in appearances and order."

The two women looked at each other and nodded. "We would be glad to have the library here," said Ruth. "And it would mean that we would get first choice of the books, wouldn't it?"

Ruth, Ingeburg, and Lutie laughed together.

"I see that you have a space here on the side which might be perfect for the chest," said Lutie.

"We could move a shelf to make a bit more

room," Ingeburg said, sizing up the area.

"I will have a box delivered to you from the coach immediately," said Lutie, "and I will relieve Mr. Mullinghurst and his family of their obligation. On my next visit, I will bring stamped cards for the school, to advertise the library there."

Lutie made quick work of the change. She promised Ingeburg and Ruth that she would return soon with another library, and she waved good-bye as the stagecoach pulled away.

This farm house held a traveling library.

WISCONSIN HISTORICAL SOCIETY, #29425

In her regular reports to the Library Commission, Lutie often wrote about difficulties that she experienced working with libraries. She wrote about the sloppiness, laziness, and rudeness that she sometimes encountered. For example, one woman opened a box of books sent to her, took out what she wanted, and then handed the package back to the express company, refusing to pay the charges either way. Sometimes books were returned in poor condition, or librarians showed little enthusiasm or interest in their work.

But just as often, Lutie wrote about the successes that sustained her. She commended librarians who oversaw flourishing libraries. She praised towns that had substantial book circulation. She noted the opening of new libraries with pride. In one report, she wrote:

"We received a letter from J.D. Bird, a prominent lumberman (from Wausaukee), *stating that the date for the opening of a library had been advertised, and we had only 10 days to purchase, ship, and prepare for circulation, 1000 volume…The state library organizer and I put in long hours to prepare the books for circulation. It was Mr. Bird, however, who gave us some unique as well as valuable assistance. Mounted on his white horse, he rode up and down the village streets calling for volunteers to help us in the library. Dozens*

of women from the community came to our aid, and the library was ready for use on the day originally designated for opening the building."

Lutie had many responsibilities in the Library Commission office in Madison. She helped to choose books to include in the traveling library chests, and she made sure the books were in good condition. She gave advice and guidance to readers and librarians around the state. She helped to put together special traveling libraries for orphanages and tuberculosis sanatoriums. She kept statistics on book circulation, wrote reports for the Legislature, and oversaw the state funding for her program.

In 1904, Wisconsin's State Capitol building burned down, and many of the records, papers, and books of the Library Commission were lost. The very next day, Lutie began to recreate lost files from memory, and to rebuild the collection of books that made up the traveling libraries. She wrote letters asking for books and money from people around the state. Although most of the files were lost, more traveling libraries were quickly reconstructed and sent out again.

In 1897, the Commission printed a booklet to publicize traveling libraries.

Spreading
the Good Word

young woman in a dark blue dress stood in a hotel lobby. As Lutie came down the stairs, the woman smiled and held out her hand. "Miss Stearns, I am Mabel Norris, the program committee chair. We are so honored that you have traveled all the way from Wisconsin to address us today. Did you sleep well?"

"Q-q-quite well, thank you. It is my pleasure to be here."

"Let me show you the ballroom where you will be speaking."

Lutie followed Miss Norris to a large banquet hall. Waiters were busy setting silverware and glasses on the tables. Soon librarians from many states would fill the room as they gathered for their annual meeting.

"You will speak to our members following our

breakfast. I will make certain that the plates are cleared away, so that there will be no distractions. I know how much we all are anticipating your speech. Your reputation as an advocate and as a speaker grows stronger every year."

"You are too kind, my dear," said Lutie. "I only hope I can be helpful in our goal of bringing books to everyone."

"Indeed," said Miss Norris. "This is why we do what we do. You will be seated at the head table. I must excuse myself, but please make yourself comfortable, and let me know if you need anything."

Lutie walked to the podium, which was on a small raised platform. She arranged her notes and looked out over the empty space. She took a deep breath as she imagined the audience that would arrive soon, to hear her speak.

Lutie ran the traveling library program in Wisconsin, but she was also active in library work around the country. As early as 1896, Melvil Dewey asked her to be the managing editor of a new national publication called *Public Libraries*. However, he wanted her to change her first name, as he thought that "Lutie" sounded undignified. She refused his suggestion and the job, but she continued to contribute to periodicals and journals about library science. In 1905, she was elected second vice president of the American Library Association. She was instrumental in starting the library school at the University of Wisconsin-Madison. She also wrote a book called *Essentials in Library Administration,* which gave advice on every aspect of starting a library. Her opinions and thoughts were highly regarded by librarians everywhere. She spoke before every university library school in existence in the United States at that time, and she was often invited to address library conferences and conventions, like this one.

In the banquet hall, Lutie looked from one side to the other. Every face was turned toward her. She had been speaking for nearly an hour about her work in Wisconsin. Although she stuttered at first, she quickly fell into a rhythm that carried her along without many interruptions. As usual, once she got past the beginning, the rest went smoothly.

"The m-m-mission of the Wisconsin Free Library Commission, from the first, has been to inform, refresh, and inspire. The need is dire. One statistic tells us that 60 percent of the occupants in our insane asylums are farmers' wives, driven there by never-ending d-d-drudgery. Nonetheless, we must be careful. I knew a woman whose husband had forbidden her to read any more books, as her housework was in constant neglect due to her attention to reading."

The audience laughed.

In the first half of her speech, Lutie shared stories from early days of the traveling libraries, stories about her journeys in the north, and about the political strategizing in the Capitol. Now she was into the heart of the subject of organizing communities.

"We cannot accomplish our task alone. We come from the outside, and are often perceived as foreign to the community. Small towns are suspicious of outsiders. We can only be the initiators, the ones to guide the process, preferably from behind the scenes. Success is adequate reward; we need not hope for personal credit and gratitude.

"The people themselves must agitate to establish county systems of traveling libraries. If the supervisors can be made to realize that the people desire it, they will be much more likely to vote for it than if the matter is presented by a Commission worker alone.

"For example, in La Crosse County in western Wisconsin, I remember how our success was due to the fact that Miss Smith, the La Crosse librarian and I first secured the cooperation of the local library board, the mayor of La Crosse, the influential 20th Century Club, the county superintendent of schools, the county judge, and other interested citizens throughout the county. Without such broad support, we would surely have failed.

"We must work with everyone who can help: with the local women's clubs, with educators, with shopkeepers, with politicians, and with whomever else might care about books.

"Do not expect that the way will be smooth. The obstacles are many. Ignorance, small-town politics, laziness, prejudice, greed, and a host of other afflictions may work to thwart and obstruct us at every turn. But stamina and constancy have their rewards.

"Let me read directly from one of my weekly reports.

"I devoted the greater part of a week to the successful attempt to secure a traveling library system for Chippewa County. The discouragements attendant upon this effort could fill a volume.

1. *The sick absentee member, who was to have introduced the resolution*
2. *the failure of promised cooperation*
3. *the postponement of consideration*
4. *when introduced, the reference of the measure to the committee on education whose chairman was the measure's strongest opponent*
5. *the open opposition of the county superintendent of schools*

6. *the neglect of the local library representative to appear in the measure's behalf*

7. *the absence of all interested, save Mrs. Porter and your humble servant*

Mrs. Porter accepted my invitation to speak and proved a tower of strength in overcoming opposition and indifference."

Lutie paused after mentioning each difficulty involved, and the audience laughed as the list grew longer. Lutie put the report down and continued.

"Persistence, my friends. Persistence in the cause. We may encounter problems, delays, resistance, and even betrayal, but always we must persevere with our eyes on the goal. Don't give up when failure seems to have swallowed your hopes, but rather return another day and try again."

Lutie looked at her notes for a moment and then slowly swept her eyes across the room.

"We d-d-dream of a world without hunger, without corruption, without violence. We work for a world of love and cooperation and enlightened thought. We hope for a world where our children learn tales of triumph rather than live stories of suffering, where our businesses consider the right action rather than the most profitable one, and where our governments consider the common good rather than the lowest common denominator. This world that calls us can only come about through changes in men's hearts. For this change, we need education, we need learning, and we need opportunity and access for everyone. There is no better example of this good world I am describing than a library, filled with knowledge and history and story and beauty, free and open to all. And not one library, but many. It is after all n-n-not the few great libraries but the 1,000 small ones that may do the most for the people. This is our goal, my friends and colleagues, and we will build it, from the state to the county to the town to the village to the hamlet to the tiny railroad outpost, where a book is handed to a child with a simple yet solemn charge; read this, and return it, so that it may be passed on, again and again and again, to lift our eyes to a better world that beckons to each of us from the words we find on the printed page.

"Thank you for your work, for your attention, and for your t-t-time."

The audience rose as one into a standing ovation when Lutie stepped back from the podium. She stood in the waves of applause for a few moments, then walked to the head table and sat down. Mrs. Norris reached out and shook Lutie's hand. The clapping slowly subsided as Lutie accepted thanks from those seated near her.

She planned on remaining at the convention for two days, but even as the room grew quiet, Lutie was thinking of her return trip to Wisconsin. She had more work to do.

A comfortable library in Dunnville.

A Life in Paper

utie Stearns sat in her office in Madison, surrounded by boxes and folders filled with reports, letters, statistics, and magazines. Today, September 4, 1914, was her last day with the Wisconsin Free Library Commission. Lutie organized loose papers and straightened file folders, making certain that her records were in order for her successor.

Lutie had worked for the Commission for nearly 20 years. Since 1895, she had helped to establish more than 150 free libraries, 1,400 traveling libraries, and 14 county library systems. She had given thousands of book talks, attended hundreds of meetings, and traveled more miles than she could possibly count, delivering books to the farthest corners of the state. Any town that could afford a library had one. In 1912 Congress authorized the post office to deliver books, so that by 1914, Lutie no longer needed to bring books to towns herself.

Many years of traveling had taken a toll on her. Though she continued to live in Milwaukee, most of her time was spent on the road or working in Madison. Her mother and sister had died the previ-

Distribution of libraries in Wisconsin around 1899. From 1899 Wisconsin Annual Report

ous year, and soon after that, Lutie had a nervous breakdown. She spent months recuperating, recovering from exhaustion, grief, and digestive problems. Lutie later said that the main reason she left her job was that she could not "*bear to return home*

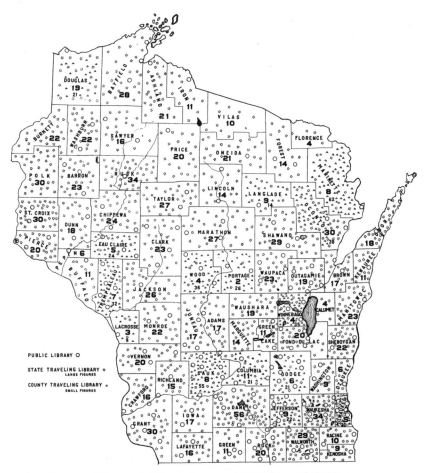

Distribution of libraries in Wisconsin around 1911. From 1912 Wisconsin Annual Report

and not find my mother there, and I needed a change of scene."

Lutie was ready for a change. Frank Hutchins, James Stout and others who had shared the initial enthusiasm for libraries were gone, and Lutie's job had become more bureaucratic and routine. She was tired of tending to administrative details in her office. But she was also ready to reach out to a larger world. She saw opportunities to address the issues of her day and age, and the work with the Library Commission had become too restrictive for her wide-ranging vision.

Lutie heard doors closing in the hall, as people left to go home for the night. She pulled a typewritten sheet of paper at random from the top file on a stack and began to read. It was one of her reports from 1906.

"*...in the crowded condition of the room, amid the buzz of excitement, more interested folk one never saw. Seventy-four books were issued, together with a quantity of magazines. One small boy proudly announced that every member of his family had a book - his father, mother, two brothers, and a baby sister. Fourteen German books were taken by those who could not read English, while a call for Danish books could not be supplied...The people remained long to*

Pick up your mail and pick up a
book at the same time in Colfax.

*talk over the books, and it was late when we started on
our 22-mile return trip.*

*Miss Elliot and I expressed sincere regret that we
could not remain and look into the homes to see the
enjoyment of old and young in the newfound treas-
ures. We left a number of books for purposes of
exchange, thus establishing the 19th station in the
county."*

She remembered the day clearly, and she remembered the boy, with his long red hair and dirty face. His excitement was as real to her in this distant room as it had been years earlier, in the crowded Grange hall. She closed her eyes and gave herself over to memories. She saw the face of a woman nearly in tears as Lutie handed her a book in German; the woman hadn't held a book in her native language for more than 23 years. She saw a war veteran reading about Lincoln and a tall teenage girl taking home a magazine about fashion in New York. Immigrant farmers, girls, boys, lumberjacks and their wives, sweaty factory workers, toddlers hanging around their mothers' skirts, storekeepers, and teachers paraded through her memory. Each one held a book in their hands.

She replaced the report. Several traveling libraries were stacked in the corner, waiting to be delivered. She noticed that a hinge on one of the chests was broken. Someone else would have to see to it.

She saw files of letters and reports with statistics. Everything neatly in its place. A life's work, in paper. Lutie picked up her bag, turned off the light, stepped into the hall and closed the door behind her.

One Strong Voice

utie Stearns left the Wisconsin Free Library Commission at age 48 to become a freelance lecturer, speaking throughout the United States and in Europe on behalf of world peace, education, and women's right to vote. She considered herself a pacifist and a radical, even as she worked within the structures of her society.

Soon after World War I, on a visit to New York City, Lutie became a Quaker. She shared the Quaker concern with social justice and non-violence, and she disliked most religions' *"pomp, ritual, and stone edifices…in excess of a congregation's needs,"* which the Quakers also rejected.

Between 1914 and 1935, her lecture tours took her to 38 different states. Her lecture titles included:

"The Education of Head, Hand, and Heart"; "Re-creation versus Wreck-creation"; "Regulate Your Hurry." Everywhere she went people wanted her to return.

She spoke about equality. "*My ruling passion is justice for all sorts and conditions of men, women, and children of any race, color or creed…No human being has the right to domination over the life of another soul even though employed by or related to him. I believe that there should be service for humanity and not profits out of the poor for things absolutely required to sustain life.*"

She spoke against racism. "*The greatest single cause of wars has been the belief of the white race that it is superior to other peoples.*"

She lectured and wrote in favor of Prohibition. When her father worked at the Soldiers' Home she had seen the damage that alcohol caused among veterans, and all her life she was convinced of the evils of drinking.

Lutie spoke on behalf of equal rights for women. She often worked with women's clubs, and was an early member of the Women's International League for Peace and Freedom, which Jane Addams organized in 1915. Her interest in women's rights had begun at an early age. When she was 10, Lutie gave a passionate speech to her friends from the top of

Lutie in 1915, soon after leaving the Commission.

her backyard woodshed, promoting women's right to vote. However, she had to wait 44 more years to see that right enacted.

Lutie never married. She wrote a book called *Books of Interest and Consolation to Spinsters.* At the end of the book she wrote, *"I'd rather not be married and be sorry I wasn't than be married and sorry I was."*

She sympathized with poor people, writing, *"I am less interested in the price of diamonds than I am in the price of milk in a baby's bottle."* Lutie had seen firsthand the hunger and poverty that many children and families suffered, and she helped raise money in Milwaukee for programs that provided food and health care. She believed that the people should own the businesses that provided for their basic needs, such as light, heat, water, and telephone.

Lutie overcame her stutter so well that her speeches became models of oratory, and she was compared to the greatest speaker of her time, William Jennings Bryan. She discovered that her stutter was worse with words that began with L, T, D, N and M, especially when they came in the beginning of a sentence. Lutie wrote her speeches out and found synonyms for words that began with those letters. Her many years of speaking before countless crowds gave her the practice she needed to improve. But her stutter never completely went away.

Lutie became friends with many famous people of her time, including Jane Addams, who created the field of social work, author Zona Gale, and progressive politician Robert M. LaFollette. After a conversation with Belle Case, Robert LaFollette's wife, Lutie became the second subscriber to *The Progressive*, a national political magazine that is still published.

Lutie was a regent at the Milwaukee State Normal College, her alma mater. She continued working with the American Library Association. She wrote books and articles about libraries, social change, and education. Lutie penned a weekly column called *"As a Woman Sees It"* that appeared in the Milwaukee Sentinel newspaper from 1932 to 1935. She continued to advocate for libraries and access to books in her frequent lectures at universities, library schools, and conventions.

During the Depression in the 1930s, Lutie's speaking engagements fell off. Her health deteriorated. She spent the last eight years of life mostly supported by one of her sisters. She lived alone and refused to go to what she called an "old ladies home."

Lutie Stearns died on December 25, 1943, in Milwaukee, Wisconsin. She was 77 years old.

Next time you go into a library, remember Lutie Stearns. Whisper her name. Lutie Stearns was one of the unseen hands that filled the shelves with books. Through her work, and the work of many others, books, once a rare and expensive commodity, are available to all of us for free.

When Frank Hutchins retired from the Library Commission in 1904, Lutie quoted Hugo Black in a farewell letter to describe her feelings about Hutchins and his work. The words she chose might as easily apply to her.

"At the end of life we shall not be asked how much pleasure we had in it but how much service we gave in it: not how full it was of success but how full it was of sacrifice, not how happy we were but how helpful we were, not how ambition was gratified, but how Love was served, for Life is judged by Love and Love is known by its fruits."

Lutie spread books like seeds, and the fruit of her labor, and her love, still nourishes us all.

CHRONOLOGY

1866	Lutie Stearns born in Stoughton, Massachusetts on September 13.
1871	Lutie's family moves to Milwaukee, Wi.
1886	Lutie graduates from State Normal School and begins teaching at Milwaukee 13th Ward School.
1888	Milwaukee Public Library hires Lutie as school liaison.
1891	Wisconsin Library Association formed.
1894	Wisconsin Library Association elects Lutie secretary-treasurer.
1895	Wisconsin Legislature passes law creating Wisconsin Free Library Commission.
1897	Lutie and Frank Hutchins become first staff people of Wisconsin Free Library Commission.
1903	Department of Traveling Libraries created with Lutie as its chief.
1904	Frank Hutchins resigns from Commission. Capitol burns in Madison.
1905	American Library Association elects Lutie second vice-president.
1912	Congress authorizes parcel post delivery for books through the U.S. Post Office
1914	Lutie leaves the Wisconsin Free Library Commission on September 4.
1914-35	Lutie lectures in United States and Europe.
1932-35	Lutie writes her column "As A Woman Sees It" for the Milwaukee Sentinel newspaper.
1943	Lutie Stearns dies in Milwaukee on December 25.

BIBLIOGRAPHY

Danton, Emily Miller, editor. *Pioneering Leaders in Librarianship.* Chicago, American Library Association, 1953

Hutchins, Frank. *Free Traveling Libraries in Wisconsin: the Story of their Growth, Purposes, and Development, with Accounts of a Few Kindred Movements.* Madison: Wisconsin Free Library Commission, 1897.

Legler, Henry. *Books for the People.* Milwaukee, Wi. 1908.

Pawley, Christine. "Advocate for Access: Lutie Stearns and the Traveling Libraries of the Wisconsin Free Library Commission, 1895-1914." *Libraries and Culture,* Volume 35, Number 3, Summer 2000, University of Texas Press.

Stearns, Lutie. *Books of Interest and Consolation to Spinsters.* 1904.

Stearns, Lutie. *Essentials in Library Administration.* ALA, 1905.

Stearns, Lutie. "My Seventy-five Years: Parts 1, 2 and 3." *Wisconsin Magazine of History* 41, 42, 43, 1959.

Stearns, Lutie E. *Traveling Libraries in Wisconsin, with directory of stations.* Madison, Wisconsin, Free Library Commission, 1910.

Tannenbaum, Earl. "The Library Career of Lutie Eugenia Stearns." *Wisconsin Magazine of History* 39, 1956.

Wiegand, Wayne. *Irrepressible Reformer: The Library Career of Melvil Dewey.* ALA, 1996.

Wilcox, Benton H. *The Wisconsin Library Association.* Madison, Wisconsin Library Association, 1966

Library Visitor Reports. WFLC, Series 1108, Box 1, Series 1112, Box 18, Series 1076, Box 18, Wisconsin Historical Society archives.

Biennial reports. Wisconsin Free Library Commission, 1896-1916, Wisconsin Historical Society archives.

APPENDIX 1

Here is a list of typical contents of one traveling library from Dunn County.

Oman's History of Greece

Hopkins' Experimental Science

Higgins' English History for Americans

Robinson Crusoe

Hans Brinker

Merchant of Venice

Sherlock Holmes

Last of the Mohicans

Alice's Adventures in Wonderland

Ivanhoe

Twice Told Tales

Wreck of the Grosvenor

Charles O'Malley

Ramona

A War-Time Wooing

A Singular Life

Hope Begham

Oakleigh

Cruise of the Canoe Club

Little Jarvis

Bird's Christmas Carol

In the Child's World

My Arctic Journal

Camps in the Rockies

Boy Traveler in the Holy Land

LaSalle

The Story of Norway

Famous American Statesmen

First Principles of Agriculture

Cyclopedia of Games and Sports

Boston Cookbook

Ivory King

Among the Love Makers

Franklin Square Song Book #1

St. Nicholas magazine

APPENDIX 2

Instructions to volunteer librarians from Senator Stout, printed inside each of the Dunn County Traveling Libraries

J.H. Stout
Menomonie, Wisconsin

The usefulness and ultimate success of these libraries will depend largely upon your efforts. The books are suited to various tastes and people should not stop taking books because they do not happen to enjoy the first they take. The criticisms of your patrons and your own reading will soon enable you to help your neighbors in their selections. The best of the books for children are enjoyed by everybody. You can get hold of some families of children with the St. Nicholas magazines who would not think of coming for them unless it was suggested to them.

Anybody can get trained readers to take interesting books. Your success will be determined by your ability to train persons who are not habitual readers of good books to become so. Be patient and do not be disappointed if you do not always secure immediate results. Things that grow slowly last the longest.

Help to train people to handle books carefully and to keep them clean, remembering always that clean hands are necessary to keep clean books. If each patron will keep his book clean all will have a continuous supply of clean books. It is much easier to teach this cleanliness and carefulness while the books are new than when they become soiled. Many people will do well to cover the books they read.

This experiment in furnishing books to small communities is being watched with interest in many places where there is more doubt as to the good care of the books and the length of time they will wear than to other points. If the experience of Dunn county shows that the people appreciate the libraries and learn to take good care of them it will encourage the establishment of such libraries in other places. Children especially should be cautioned to use great care in handling the books. Good care of books should not, however, be harped upon till people are afraid to use them. The formation of right habits is more valuable than the saving of the money involved. Take the people into your confidence in this matter and they will be glad to aid you.

In sending out libraries, preference will be given to the communities which return them in the best condition.

Please have books stand straight on the shelves or lie flat on their sides. In returning libraries pack the books so securely that they will not slide or shift. If leaves of books become loose do not re-issue the books but keep them in your possession till the library is returned. If any of your patrons persist in soiling the books unduly, refuse to loan to them until you have written…for instructions. The cost of each book is shown on the list on the door of the case. For lost books collect its cost and for undue damage collect a fair portion of the cost.

You will confer a favor by making any suggestions…on the increased usefulness of these libraries.

A catalogue of the Memorial Library is sent upon request…(containing) books of the latter to cultivate a desire for wider reading in special lines of interest…books are free to all residents of Dunn county.

Finally in all cases of doubt, remember (the purpose) of the Traveling Libraries and of the Memorial Library is "to do the greatest good for the most people."

Yours unto
death, + after
Lutie E. Stearns
aug, 1915.

I found the picture on page 85 while I was researching Lutie at the State Historical Society. It was printed on a postcard, (which was a common practice in those days), and on the back I read this inscription, which says, *"Yours unto death, and after, Lutie E. Stearns."*

I felt like Lutie was sending a secret message through the ages to me, and to all of us who love books and who carry on her work in our own ways.

Who was she really writing to?

We'll never know; it's a mystery.